PRP

A Roadmap for Success©

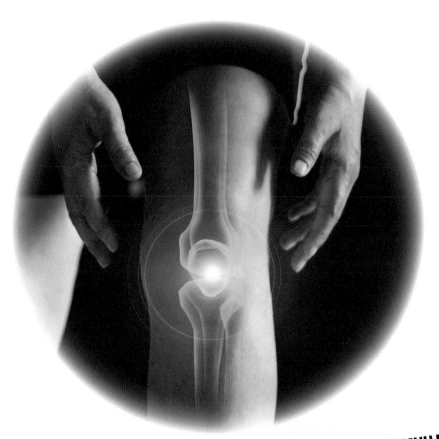

Kevin Edward Elder,

Asailor onboard an ocean-going vessel in the 1500s-1600s was limited regarding medical care when the need arose. A good ship surgeon was one who was quickest with the saw to amputate an ailing limb, using limited anesthesia, likely in the form of heavy doses of Grog.

Fast forward a couple 100 years, and even simple infections and other medical conditions were still treated based on basic ideas and techniques that we would find laughable or shocking with our current medical knowledge. For example, George Washington's doctors treated his throat infection with severe bloodletting, an enema, molasses, and burning/blistering his throat (which obviously made him even worse).

Fortunately, science and the advancement of medical treatments continues to grow at an exciting rate of change. For the patient with osteoarthritis, or as patients often say, "old age arthritis", the end of the road may well be a joint replacement. This valuable treatment may dramatically change the life of the patient with end-stage arthritis. However, it is not an option without risks, and many patients do not have a level of osteoarthritis that would warrant joint replacement surgery yet. What do these patients do? Steroid injections or "cortisone injections" have been performed since the 1950s, with the first product commercially available around 1948-1949. For a long time, these

> **F**ast forward a couple 100 years, and even simple infections and other medical conditions were still treated based on basic ideas and techniques that we would find laughable or shocking with our current medical knowledge.

treatments were the only option for treatment of osteoarthritis pain and dysfunction. Cortisone injections are short lasting treatments that also carry a certain level of risk. Elevation of blood sugars, short-term overall relief, and decline of the joint condition are a few concerns that arise with this treatment. In fact, some recent studies document actual worsening of osteoarthritis of the knee with repetitive steroid injections as compared to placebo/saline injections of the knee when done repetitively over a period of years.

Many other patients will resort to anti-inflammatories/NSAIDs such as ibuprofen, Motrin, Aleve, and various prescription versions as an adjunctive treatment to try and manage their pain. This class of medications is known to have many risks:

Risks/problems with anti-inflammatories
- Gastrointestinal issues such as ulcers and gastritis
- Cardiovascular risks, such as hypertension, increased rates of congestive heart failure and an increase in risk of heart attack and stroke, issues of increased edema
- Kidney damage and compromise–especially in older patients,
- All of these risks despite not actually doing anything to slow or change the course of the osteoarthritis itself.
- Recent studies show evidence of slowing of bone healing in animal models; in the case of fractures, this brings even further questions to the table about this class of medications.

   **In addition, these medications also carry a financial cost besides their medical risks. When factoring in the costs of medical issues there is quite a significant overall cost of these medications.

Natural anti-inflammatories and special diets may have a role and have less risks associated when used appropriately. Patients with inflammatory types of arthritis may benefit, especially from anti-inflammatory diets, but the data behind some of these treatments

66To say this is a hot area in the field of sports medicine is a massive understatement. 99

are limited. In addition, the cost of some of the supplements can also be quite significant over time.

There is a lot of recent information and interest in **CBD derivatives**, and this may present an additional adjunctive option for patients, however much of the research is still in process. As with any natural or nutraceutical type compound it is imperative that care is taken to try and identify the best possible source of these compounds and try to do all that one can to avoid unnecessary toxicity or contaminants.

More recent treatments include hyaluronic acid injections, or "chicken shots" / "rooster comb shots" as I have heard patients call them. Not all **hyaluronic acid injections** are avian derived (some are synthetic). These injections exist in various preparations. This may include a singular large injection to as many as 5 injections, typically done one week between each shot. They certainly offer an alternative to steroid injections, and may have some benefit for some patients, however some studies question their overall benefit as compared to placebo or saline. In my clinical practice I have used these injections for many years and I do find that they have a role, especially in a patient whom is not getting adequate relief from steroid injections, and is trying to delay joint replacement, or maybe is not a medical candidate for joint replacement. However, the next set of injections, the subject of this book, has been compared directly in head-to-head comparison with hyaluronic acid and has shown superior results.

These latest treatments are from the orthobiologic realm: **platelet rich plasma, and so-called "stem cell" preparations.** What many people will refer to as "stem cell" injections are cellular injections derived from either bone marrow or adipose (fat tissue) that contain some amounts of mesenchymal stem cells, but these are not pure preparations of stem cells, which is often a point of confusion. Other preparations such as amniotic or placental derivatives exist as well. These preparations of amniotic and placental derivatives are often freeze-dried or dehydrated, so they are not live cells and by definition are not stem cells. They do not contain any live cells.

To say this is a hot area in the field of sports medicine is a massive understatement. Patients, when faced with poor solutions such as repetitive steroid injections and/or chronic anti-inflammatory (NSAID) use, experience significant decline in their daily function and significant pain levels. Many of these patients are looking for better alternatives.

We will wade into these waters and provide some direction to this landscape on this journey, PRP: A Roadmap for Success. In the emerging fields of science, there is constantly new information coming out that can influence the direction of treatments and provide better clarity and reasoning for what has been observed from prior experience.

In order to embark upon a journey, it is good to have an understanding of where one is going; have a concept of how one hopes to get there (the route/plan for the journey ahead) and reasonable expectations of what may be encountered on the journey as well at journey's end: That is to say the end result. PRP: A Roadmap for Success has been written with this philosophy in mind.

About the Author:

Kevin Edward Elder, MD, FAAFP, CAQSM, is an experienced physician practicing in Tampa Bay, Florida. He received his undergraduate degree at The Ohio State University (B.S., Microbiology), and subsequently attended medical school at the University of Toledo in Ohio. He was voted by his classmates to be the graduation commencement speaker for his graduating class. After finishing Family Medicine residency at Bayfront Medical Center in St. Petersburg, Florida, where he was a chief resident in his 3rd year, he completed a Sports Medicine fellowship also at Bayfront Medical Center.

He is in practice in Tampa Florida, treating adult and pediatric Sports Medicine patients, and is board certified in Sports Medicine and Family Medicine. He has extensive experience with musculoskeletal ultrasound and was one of the first physicians in the area performing this diagnostic evaluation on patients, as well as one of the first physicians in the area performing PRP. He has lectured extensively on this topic and has several publications in this area as well. He has performed over 3000 PRP injections and continues to work on perfecting the process.

Dr. Elder has significant team Sports Medicine experience, having covered a variety of high school, collegiate, and professional sports, including serving as Team Physician for the Tampa Bay Buccaneers for 5 years.

He currently works as a Team Physician for U.S. Soccer as well as the U.S. Ski Team, and a couple of local high schools in Tampa. He has traveled to several countries to support the U.S. Ski Team, and has covered various events for U.S. Soccer, including being named Team Physician Coordinator for the U23M/Olympic Team. He also presently serves as an assistant team physician for the Tampa Bay Rays and University of South Florida and provides Sports Medicine consultations for the Tampa Bay Rowdies soccer team and Tampa Bay Lightning. In addition, he also covered various sporting events in the Tampa Bay area, including triathlons, and has served as Medical Liaison for various sporting events including the Gold Cup, ACC Championship Game, and other events, including Team Doctor for Chicken Creek Ranch.

Former Team Physician for the Tampa Bay Buccaneers, Dr. Kevin Elder, MD, FAAFP.

Dr. Kevin Elder seen during his time with the Tampa Bay Buccaneers.

With any new area of discovery, there is always a lot of questions that arise. This is certainly the case in new fields of science. Many times, the process of discovery follows a route: First there is disbelief or detractors – many questioning the validity of any deviation from the normal pattern and protocols. Thereafter, there may be a period of discovery and then subsequently acceptance. And after some time, this once unusual and questioned treatment becomes the new normal.

In many ways, the field of Orthobiologics/cellular therapy has followed this route. Throughout this time, there will be need to guard against false advertising and promises, and as always it is important to critically examine facts and experience. When defining success, it is important to understand what the expected and realistic outcomes may be and vital that patients are presented with realistic expectations. The ethics of this field of study have been defined here:

https://orthobioethics.com/the-orthobiologic-ethics-statement/

This writing is not meant to be a definitive step-by-step instruction manual, however, an attempt has been made to provide the best evidence as it is presently defined, combined with the extensive experience of the author.

Dr. Kevin Elder (far left) is a current team physician with U.S. soccer.

Disclaimer: The opinions described herein are those of the author personally, and do not necessarily reflect the opinions of the author's medical group. This book is not intended to take the place of any medical evaluation, which should be done by a licensed professional clinician qualified in the field of sports medicine/orthopedics/rheumatology. Nothing in this book is intended as individual medical advice. Any treatment should be secondary to a proper work-up and evaluation, not arranged through a seminar. All treatments should take into account the patient's medical history and involve appropriate discussion of risks, benefits, options, and realistic expectations of treatment. Any work-up and evaluation is an individualized process and involves individualized medical attention and decision making. Neither the author nor the publisher may be held liable for any damage, loss, or injury sustained by anyone who relies solely on the information provided in this book or on information from websites, articles, books, organizations, or any other medical practitioners or research which may be mentioned in this book. No person associated with this book is responsible for patients who decide to seek help from an insufficiently trained physician in the field of Orthobiologics/cellular therapy.

PRP

YOU ARE HERE

WHAT IS IT?

To begin, we must first start with a review of what PRP actually is. PRP is derived from the patient's own blood (autologous). It is derived by taking a small sample of blood and then spinning this down in the centrifuge to separate the whole blood into red blood cells, platelet poor plasma and the platelet rich plasma or "buffy coat". Various commercial preparations exist that result in various platelet concentrations. At present, most clinicians consider platelet rich plasma to have a platelet concentrate containing at least 4-6 times that of baseline values in the final sample. This layer of "buffy coat", having been obtained from the centrifuge process, is then extracted from the separated mixture and injected into the target area.

HOW DOES IT WORK?

When platelets are injected into the targeted area of a tendon, muscle, or joint – the platelets activate, releasing growth factors. It is these growth factors that lead to the beneficial properties of platelet rich plasma.

Some of these growth factors include:
- platelet derived growth factor
- epithelial growth factor
- fibroblast growth factor
- transforming growth factor beta
- vascular endothelial growth factor

All these various growth factors have different roles which include:
- helping with muscle, tendon, connective tissue healing
- stimulating growth of blood vessels
- attracting macrophages which are cleaning up cellular debris
- stimulating connective tissue growth
- stimulating formation of collagen
- stimulating formation of new blood vessels
- promoting healing

Various other inter-molecular signaling takes place from cytokines and interleukins. These proteins/molecules help with molecular signaling, promoting repair.

WHAT PRP IS NOT

PRP is not "stem cells", which we will discuss separately later. PRP can have several positive effects when it is injected appropriately, but it should not be advertised or thought of as "stem cell therapy". PRP is not a "cure" for arthritis. It has been shown to have positive benefits in various conditions, but no treatment is always guaranteed to work. PRP may have some effect on slowing down the progression of arthritis, but a lot of studies and work still needs to be done to better define the exact properties. PRP can benefit some patients experiencing pain from arthritis by decreasing pain, improving function, and/or decreasing or eliminating the need for anti-inflammatory medications which have known toxicities and risks. It does have far and away the best evidence behind it as compared to other treatments in this field of study. We will talk about that in more detail in the sections to follow.

There are studies of patients treated for knee arthritis that appeared to have some delay in the progression of arthritis. Just like putting plant fertilizer down on a field, there will be likely a need to repeat the treatments down the road, especially in the case of arthritis for example. It is also important to note the PRP does not, for example, magically reconnect a completely torn ACL or reconnect a completely torn rotator cuff.

WHAT CONDITIONS CAN BE TREATED WITH PRP?

Many conditions are treated by PRP. It is used to treat arthritis of various joints, including knees, hips, shoulders, ankle, thumb and foot joints for example. It is also used to treat various tendon injuries and muscle injuries. As with many beneficial treatments, the "devil is in the details." Just because PRP has good data behind its use for some types of arthritis and tendon injuries does not mean it will work the same for every condition or should be used with every injury. In this regard, our discussion will focus on what has been currently reported or what has been the experience of this author in treating patients over 8+ years and over 3000 injections of PRP in a variety of conditions.

There are definitely some areas that are less clear but may be promising in nature, while others seem to be dead ends or are in the realm of fantasy. The idea, for example, that the patient might be cured of diabetes by receiving injections of PRP into the bloodstream is neither logical nor proven in any capacity. PRP is also used for various cosmetic purposes (e.g. "vampire facials") but these other treatments are not the practice area of this author and therefore will not be discussed here.

UNDERSTANDING THE PATH/READING THE TERRAIN

Understanding why PRP might be used for tendon/muscle injuries requires understanding tendons themselves. Tendons are what attach muscles to bone. Unlike the "meat" of the muscle, tendons do not have great blood supply. They are also under high tension/demand. These factors not only make tendons susceptible to injury, but also slow to heal when injured. The body responds to an injury by creating an inflammatory response. The inflammatory response brings blood flow and thus certain cells involved in the repair of an injury to the injury site. When a tendon is chronically injured over the course of a long period of time, negative results that further impede healing may occur, such as formation of scar, or even calcifications within the tendon, often at the tendon insertion on the bone. This is sometimes referred to as calcific tendinitis. Also, actual spurs may be seen extending into the tendon itself. These calcifications sometimes can get so large they are seen on x-ray.

Examples

- Plantar fasciitis "heel spurs" on the bottom/plantar aspect of the foot
- Achilles tendon "heel spurs" at the back of the heel
- Kneecap/patellar spurs from the quadriceps tendon or patellar tendon
- Calcifications in the rotator cuff

Calcifications may themselves cause pain with movement of the affected area, and they also affect the movement or elasticity of the area. It is like a fresh rubber band versus one that has grown less elastic and broken down from being left out in the sun. Not only does the rubber band not stretch or move as well, but it may actually snap apart! Scar within the tendon is not of the same elasticity as the tendon itself, meaning it does not stretch in the same way. These issues all tend to compound because they affect the movement not only of the extremity, but the whole body. This is referred to as the kinetic chain.

RESPECTING THE ELEMENTS: THE KINETIC CHAIN

Just as a traveler should take into account the elements and weather conditions when departing on a journey, with musculoskeletal conditions we must account for the kinetic chain. The kinetic chain is essentially the effect of movement (or dis-coordinated movement because of injury or disuse) into other corresponding areas, much like a weak link in a chain affects the strength of the whole chain itself.

A sports specific example would be a baseball pitcher with a foot injury to his planting foot. He may have a strong upper body and spine, but when he is trying to plant his foot, he is unable to do so effectively, so may compensate by changing his natural motion, leading to ineffective mechanics, or further injuries up the kinetic chain.

Another example would be a volleyball player who has a rotator cuff injury. She may compensate by changing the rotation of her overhead striking, thus relying on other muscles in the corresponding area such as the trapezius muscles and place even more strain on her neck or upper back. In addition to loss of function and strength in her arm, she may begin to encounter neck or back stiffness, or even pain in the opposite shoulder from relying more on it.

Remember how hours spent hunched over with bad posture causes neck or back stiffness? Or how tight hamstrings, combined with weak core muscles may contribute to increased back pain?

Like a car out of alignment, these issues must always be addressed as well. In the case of the car we may have uneven wear of tires, or actual linkage vs alignment issues resulting in an uncomfortable ride or worse a "death wobble" (in the case of some large wheeled vehicles I have driven!)

In regards to the body as a whole, we may encounter further injury and decline in ability and function beyond what we would already find due to age and natural degeneration. The body is a machine. The only machine we are granted with on our journey. Unlike a car, we cannot swap out for a new model every 5 to 10 years (at least not yet... 😃).

Like a car, when we are young, we may be compared to a fresh new car gleaming driven from the lot, requiring little maintenance. But with time, we become more of a "classic" car, which still may be a beautiful muscle car or vintage car, still well capable of getting the job done! But we do know that these machines require more attention and TLC than something that is brand-new.

What is important to always remember is that injuries do not occur in a vacuum. They may often be the result of defects in the kinetic chain, or themselves cause a disruption in the kinetic chain.

Specific examples include:
- Tight calf muscles of patients with plantar fasciitis or Achilles tendon injuries
- Knee pain from poorly tracking kneecap/patella with alignment issues and/or relative weakness of certain quadriceps muscles

IF WE CORRECT KINETIC CHAIN ISSUES AND TREAT THE TENDON, CAN WE CURE/HEAL TENDON INJURIES WITH PRP?

In many cases, if PRP is done properly, and attention to details is of paramount importance *(technique!)*, we have literature describing the actual healing of some tendon injuries, and it has been the experience of the author and others experienced in this field that this can be the case.

It does not however seem that all tendon injuries may be equally responsive to PRP.

PRESENTLY, BETWEEN THE CURRENT LITERATURE AND THE AUTHORS OWN EXPERIENCE THESE WOULD BE BROKEN INTO CERTAIN CATEGORIES

When might PRP be best option/highest present evidence & good experience of author:

- Early Knee OA
- Medial collateral ligament/MCL
- Various Tendinopathy including
  - Lateral/medial epicondylitis
  - Plantar fasciitis
  - Achilles tendon
  - Rotator cuff/especially isolated cuff injuries (not full-thickness tears)
  - Hamstring/quadriceps tendinopathy
  - Gastrocnemius/calf muscle tendinopathy
  - Gluteus Medius tendinopathy (often misdiagnosed as hip bursitis)

Less published evidence/however good experience of author:

- **Some conditions may have not been as thoroughly studied, but this does not mean this is not a very good option to consider. It has been the experience of the author that these conditions responded very favorably
- De Quervain's tenosynovitis (wrist tendinitis at the top portion of the thumb)
- Hand flexor tendinopathy
- Ulnar collateral ligament partial tear
  - Details of proximal or distal, extent of tear, and timeline of the patient/athlete all very important factors in making this complicated decision

Tougher conditions/with not as much data, but still good option to consider:

- **Again not "curing arthritis", but injection of PRP may be far more favorable than steroid injections which can be very short lasting; lead to further degeneration of the joint, soft tissue atrophy or depigmentation, and elevation of blood sugars, amongst many issues. It has been the experience of the author that PRP injections may provide significant functional relief of pain, and patients sometimes get lasting relief for 12+ months for these conditions which is tremendous!
- Ankle arthritis
- Carpometacarpal/CMC arthritis (base of thumb: Most common joint in body to get arthritis)
- Hallux rigidus (arthritis of the big toe resulting in stiffness and significant pain)
- Glenohumeral arthritis (shoulder joint)
- Acromioclavicular joint arthritis ("point" of the shoulder)

The Toughest Conditions/Data is conflicting/most challenging for author also:

- Patellar tendon
  - Challenging condition, comprehensive approach required including extensive physical therapy
  - Technique may be very important, there are some papers published describing specific technique when injecting "Patellar scraping"
- Hip/labrum and hip arthritis
  - Neither the literature nor author's experience provides the same level of results in comparison to the knee arthritis.
  - Still may be the best option for patient that is not ready for surgery.

- Candid conversation a must.
- Important to make sure that the source of the pain is clearly identified, and it is not being referred from the back, or some of the muscles around the hip joints

---

Emerging Areas showing some promise:
- Peripheral nerve
  - Technique also key here, doing "hydrodissection" under MSK US to "free up" nerve from entrapment. May be additional benefit of growth factors from PRP on nerve tissue
- Spine/intradiscal
  - Technique and experience also paramount. May require use of fluoroscopy or other imaging for appropriate guidance. Often doctors who inject this area may specialize in the spine/ or do mostly spine injections

---

 PRP can "reset the clock" and kick-start the healing process.

Part of the key is that the PRP is placed accurately at the site of the injury in order to achieve the best possible result.

THE HEALING CASCADE

Understanding PRP = Understanding The Healing Cascade

Hemostasis
- Clot formation to degranulation of platelets - this involves stopping the acute bleeding

Acute Inflammatory Phase
- Can last up to 72 hours – characterized by pain, swelling, redness and increased local temperature

Intermediate Repair Phase
- 48 hours to 6 weeks
- Anatomic structures restored and tissue regeneration occurring
- Fibroblasts, angiogenesis–activity of the growth factors is seen on the tissues

Advanced Remodeling Phase
- 3 weeks to 12 months
- Collagen remodeling

In a sense, when there is a chronic injury the healing/tissue repair cascade has stalled out. Or there is an inhibition of this because of scar formation or other issues. By doing PRP we effectively restart the healing cascade, basically by directly placing a concentrate of platelets at the site of injury. These concentrated platelets degranulate. This kicks off the acute inflammatory phase, which is part of the reason why some patients will have some pain during the first couple of days after the procedure. Thereafter, the effect of the activated platelets, basically from the growth factors, are what lead to the beneficial effect of the PRP.

PRP can "reset the clock" and kick-start the healing process.

Part of the key is that the PRP is placed accurately at the site of the injury in order to achieve the best possible result.

FACTORS THAT AFFECT THE SUCCESS OF PRP:

These include:

- Which tendon/injury is being treated
- How long or how badly the tendon is injured
- Specific techniques of procuring and or performing PRP itself including the **skill of the clinician, accuracy**
- Possible "dose" of the PRP, including number of injections required to achieve the positive result
- Patient factors including
  - Age
  - Health of patient, possibly baseline platelet counts

- Type of PRP being used
- Kinetic chain issues as previously discussed
- Avoiding confounding variables which may affect the success of PRP
  - Recent anti-inflammatory use or steroid use
  - Possible inactivation or effect on the PRP by certain local anesthetics
  - Appropriate offloading and activity modification after injection

HOW IS A PRP INJECTION PERFORMED?

Here I will describe my technique:

In a sterile fashion, a small sample of your own blood is taken first. After spinning the sample down in the centrifuge, the PRP is extracted from the sample in the usual sterile fashion. Thereafter, the area of the injection is cleaned and prepared in the usual sterile fashion. Sterile gel is applied to the area.

The area of the injection is identified with musculoskeletal ultrasound. Using musculoskeletal ultrasound, the tract of the needle is injected with a local anesthetic (ropivacaine), up to the area of the injection but not into the area of the injection. This is done in order to avoid any effect on the PRP itself.

Subsequently this PRP is injected under MSK ultrasound guidance in a sterile fashion.

HOW LONG WILL IT TAKE?

Patients may be in the office for approximately an hour between checking in and departing. However, the actual procedure itself (specifically the injection) may only be a few minutes. It may be possibly longer depending on the area being injected and need for any additional needling of the injured area, after the local anesthetic has been injected, typically done in cases of chronic or severe tendinopathy. In general, in the case of a joint injection there is not a need for additional needling of the area as the injection is being performed with MSK US guidance into the joint and that is it.

IS IT PAINFUL?

PRP, like any injection involves a needle, so there may be some minor discomfort. However, the author tries to decrease this minor discomfort with topical sprays such as ethyl chloride "cold spray" and local anesthesia. This local anesthesia is specifically ropivacaine, and not others because of a concern for negative effect on the PRP. Generally, tendon injections require some needle tenotomy ("tenderizing" the muscle tendon prior to injection). These injections may be slightly more painful, however typically the discomfort comes later, after the local anesthesia wears off. In general, Tylenol may be used after the injection, and if clinically indicated, a small prescription of mild pain medication may also be written.

SAFETY

PRP is derived from the patient's own body and blood. Using usual sterile techniques and procedures, when done properly it is a procedure that has good safety data and history. Advantages are that it is autologous (from the patient's own body/blood) and thus minimizes any chance of "reaction". Any injection comes with a theoretical risk. Using MSK ultrasound to perform injections has been proven to increase the accuracy of injection, even in those physicians with many years of experience performing the injections. Increased accuracy may not only result in higher levels of success but may also result in higher degrees of safety.

WHAT TO LOOK FOR IN YOUR PHYSICIAN?

Having this or any procedure done is a big decision, and there are certain things that a patient should look for when deciding which doctor to see for an initial consultation:

- Is the doctor board certified?
- Is an appropriate workup being done/or just signing up to do injections?
- Experience of doctor? (Everyone starts somewhere, but technical skill with anything increases with time and experience. Having done hundreds of injections is much better than dozens)
- Is MSK US used for guidance of injection? (If not, it's like taking a shot in the dark - guessing where it is going)
- Is an MD/DO performing the injection? (Some clinics may recruit patients and then have a mid-level practitioner (ARNP or PA) actually performing the injections who may or may not use MSK US or have any expertise with it for that matter)
- What is the process? (an assembly line of injections with no follow-up, or are there solid follow up plans made?)
- Instructions provided/ability to ask questions?
- Familiarity of the doctor with the literature?
- Feedback from other patients/reviews?

WHAT IS THE COST OF PRP?

PRP is not presently covered by insurance companies, with some rare exceptions. There is no standard exact price of PRP, although most clinics offering true PRP treatments tend to have somewhat similar pricing, at least within the United States. This is not presently the case with pricing of what is referred to as "stem cell treatments", which seem to be a little more akin to the "Wild West". Pricing is all over the place.

"Having this or any procedure done is a big decision, and there are certain things that a patient should look for when deciding which doctor to see for an initial consultation.**"**

The total cost will depend on the number of injections that are needed, as well as the need for follow-up visits and/or physical therapy. Follow-up visits and physical therapy are typically covered by insurance. Generally speaking, the cost of PRP is a reflection of the cost of the materials being used to prepare it, the time and experience of the clinician performing it, and any other materials such as local anesthesia, as well as the use and application of MSK ultrasound for accuracy and guidance.

WHAT IS THE TRUE COST OF PRP?

The cost of PRP is an investment patients make in themselves that they are willing to make to avoid the true cost of continuing to have loss of function, and decreased quality of life.

One would have to be living in a cave underground to not be aware of the cost of the narcotic epidemic on our society and the lives of many patients and families. These medications were often used for many years in treatment of the same conditions of chronic joint pain, and muscle and tendon pain, with disastrous results. The irony is that these treatments were covered by insurance companies.

For many years, anti-inflammatories were also heavily prescribed to patients, and many patients still continue to rely on these medications in order to function in their daily lives, despite the known risks to their gastrointestinal system, kidneys, cardiovascular system and increased risk of morbidity (illness) and death. These anti-inflammatory treatments are also covered by insurance companies. Doing occasional steroid or cortisone injections may make clinical sense for certain patients to provide them relief if they do not have other good options. Doing regular steroid injections on a scheduled basis is known to be harmful to our joints however and certainly can lead to further tendon injury and degeneration. Some patients may not have any other options

> **"The cost of PRP is an investment patients make in themselves that they are willing to make to avoid the true cost of continuing to have loss of function, and decreased quality of life."**

due to certain individual factors including their medical history, cost, or other various factors. Whether or not the steroid injections are clinically best for patients, they are generally "covered" by insurance, despite the fact that they often have very little benefit, or in fact are potentially harmful.

We have discussed the benefits of doing physical therapy and rehabilitation which is vital in addressing the kinetic chain. However in a patient who has reached a plateau, or is not continuing to improve with physical therapy alone, we must ask: what is the financial cost of either giving up their physical activity and potentially having weight gain/obesity issues, or continuing to go to physical therapy and pay for office visits when there has been no further improvement. Some patients may see a variety of doctors over the course of many years and try a variety of treatments without resolution, and this also presents a significant cost.

Most importantly, what is the true cost of loss of activity and function, which may lead into a negative spiral of moving less, gaining weight and living an even more unhealthy lifestyle?

The incidence of obesity is already a sobering fact in the United States and many other countries. Along with obesity and decreased activity often comes diabetes, hypertension and elevated cholesterol. With these Horsemen of the Apocalypse come the increased risk of all-cause mortality including heart attacks as well as cancers. What is the cost of the increased pharmaceutical medications and doctor visits the patient may have to incur as a result of their decreased activity and physical decline? What is the cost of the diminished psychological sense of wellbeing that occurs because of loss of function?

Much like regenerative medicine itself, cost is a complicated topic with many variables.

The best thing a patient can do is consider all variables before making a decision. Get another opinion, especially if the answer is not clear (not from your cousin who is in training to become an assistant vet tech or from "Dr. Google" or from a seminar, but an actual doctor in the sports medicine or orthopedic field, during an actual office visit and have an actual discussion about the options.)

HOW DO I PREPARE FOR THE INJECTION?

The first step is to get a good night's sleep, stay off "Dr. Google", avoid anti-inflammatories, and drink plenty of water. In addition, it is important to eat a good breakfast. There is no restriction on food, in fact it is much preferable not to be fasting prior to the procedure.

There are theories that eating a healthier diet and avoiding an "inflammatory diet" may help provide the best result and have the best immune effect from the body. There have been entire books written on this topic and patients can reference these. It seems that certain

> **The first step is to get a good night's sleep, stay off "Dr. Google", avoid anti-inflammatories, and drink plenty of water.**

patients may respond more directly than others to these changes, however when thinking about dietary foods/fuel, as the saying goes: "garbage in = garbage out"

Examples of Simple Dietary Decisions
- Eating fruits and nuts that have less inflammatory properties may be helpful, including blueberries, apples, blackberries, raspberries, strawberries, pecans, almonds
- Choosing less meats or at least lean meats such as chicken, lamb, fresh fish, or turkey
- Drinking black coffee, herbal teas, fresh juices instead of caffeinated sodas or processed sugar-containing drinks
- Healthy, fresh vegetables
- Avoiding or limiting alcohol

Obviously quitting smoking as this has many known negative effects on the body. Hopefully someone who is considering PRP will also consider avoiding the horrible assault on the body that smoking confers.

Other Ideas To Stimulate Health:
- Improved sleep quality
  - Trying to manage stress, avoiding blue lights before bed, sleep hygiene-avoiding caffeine so there is more good quality sleep.
- Avoiding fast foods + processed foods that contain high degrees of sugar
- Avoiding high degrees of saturated fats
- Exercise is medicine...!
  - In general exercise and motion can help bring blood flow to an area, movement is important.

- Managing stress, as stress leads to cortisol release, and cortisol is a toxic hormone
- Self-care which may include meditation, yoga, prayer
- Managing any other known inflammatory conditions, for example if there's a history of inflammatory arthritis - trying to control it in consultation with other doctors/rheumatology

WHAT ARE CONTRAINDICATIONS TO PRP?

Absolute contraindications include:
- Platelet dysfunction syndrome
- Critical thrombocytopenia
- Hemodynamic instability
- Septicemia
- Local infection at the site of the procedure or open skin
- Patient unwilling to accept risks and/or costs of procedure

Relative contraindications include:
- Consistent use of NSAIDs prior to the procedure (especially within 48 hours but maybe as long as 5 days)
- Corticosteroid injection at the treatment site within 1 month
- Systemic use of steroids within 4 weeks
- Tobacco use
- Recent fever or illness
- Cancer- especially of blood or bone derived
- HgB 10 g/dl
- Platelet count < 105

ARE THERE ANY SPECIAL INSTRUCTIONS?

It is important to avoid anti-inflammatories. Restrictions on weightbearing, or relative activity restriction may all be part of the special instructions. The specific guidance will be given by your doctor and should be a part of any appropriately done procedure. Part of the importance of follow-up after the procedure is to determine the next steps. These may include physical therapy and/or determination of need for any further treatment for example. The initial follow up after PRP may be at 2 weeks after the procedure. It is important to realize that often the area of the injection may feel worse initially after the injection, especially in the case of tendon or muscle injuries, for the first couple days or even first couple weeks. PRP is a molecular process, so therefore remember to be patient. Slow and steady wins this race.

ARE THERE ANY RESTRICTIONS AFTER A PRP INJECTION?

The first step is to talk to the doctor performing your injection. Specific instructions will be provided in relation to what injection was done. Certain injections such as the Achilles tendon may require nonweightbearing with crutches for 48 hours, followed by a boot for 2 weeks. Other injections, such as the knee may not require any restriction except for relative decrease of exercise. Certainly, any anti-inflammatories should be avoided for several weeks after the injection.

WHAT ARE THE NAMES OF COMMON ANTI-INFLAMMATORIES?

Some common over-the-counter or prescription anti-inflammatories include:

• aspirin	• Voltaren	• Celebrex
• Motrin	• Advil	• Daypro
• Aleve	• ibuprofen	• Feldene
• Naprosyn	• meloxicam	• Lodine
• naproxen	• Mobic	• Ansaid

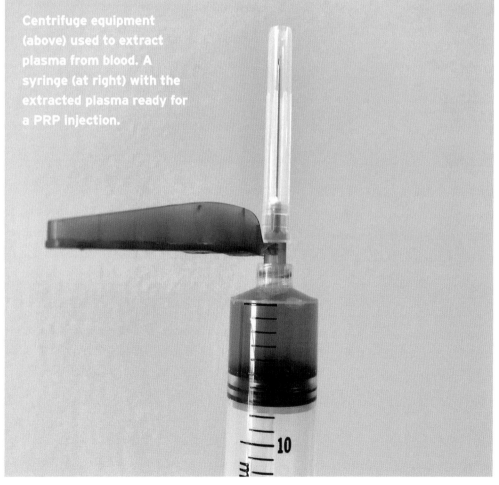

Centrifuge equipment (above) used to extract plasma from blood. A syringe (at right) with the extracted plasma ready for a PRP injection.

It is also vital that prednisone and any other corticosteroid injections are discontinued 3 weeks prior and as many as 4 weeks post the injection.

WHAT ARE THE CURRENT CONTROVERSIES OF PRP?

Some of the present controversies are:
- PRP does not work for everything!
- What are the optimal platelet counts or concentration?
- What role do white cells have regarding PRP?
  (presently it is thought that using a "white cell rich" sample is better for tendons while using a "white cell poor" is better for joints)
- What are the appropriate number of injections and the timing of these injections for each given condition?

IS THERE ONE SYSTEM THAT IS THE BEST SYSTEM FOR PRP INJECTIONS?

At present, there are many companies that have different commercial products used to prepare PRP. These products can differ in the platelet concentration, as well as the number of white cells that are present in the sample of PRP. There is much debate about what is the perfect concentration of platelets; what is the perfect concentration and type of white cells, amongst other considerations. These companies all differ in their preparation. Some doctors make their own PRP, in part so that they can adjust some of these factors according to current trends and research. It does seem that PRP which is higher in white cell count (leukocyte rich PRP) seems to be better for tendon issues whereas PRP which is lower in white cell count (leukocyte poor PRP) seems to be better for intra-articular "in the joint" applications. However, there are studies showing effectiveness of both types of injections for either conditions. In addition, there is theory that the type of white cells may play a role, with certain type of white cells (monocytes) being beneficial, however other types of white cells (neutrophils) being less beneficial, or potentially even harmful.

Certainly, this is a complicated area!

> **"At present, there is much debate about what is the perfect concentration of platelets; what is the perfect concentration and type of white cells, amongst other considerations."**

What we do understand at present is that the PRP is defined as a sample containing at least 4-6 X's the platelet concentration found in normal blood.

DOES THE BASELINE PLATELET CONCENTRATION AFFECT THE OVERALL RESULT?

The baseline platelet concentration may affect the overall result, however the exact nature of this is not well established in the literature at present. Part of this may be because if there are slight differences in the baseline platelet concentrate, when the platelets are concentrated 4-6 times baseline, there is still a significant amount of platelets in any sample. In general, if a patient has a very low platelet concentrate, it is felt that PRP may still be effective, however there may not be the same degree of result. The challenge may actually be in performing the procedure in the first place, because a platelet count that is very low leads to increased risk of bleeding. This patient may not be a candidate for PRP in the first place.

SO HOW CAN WE SOLVE SOME OF THESE PROBLEMS?

First, despite not clearly understanding what is a perfect concentration of platelets, or what are the perfect number, or timing of PRP injections; and not having any absolutely conclusive idea of what is the perfect white cell concentrate within the PRP, we still have growing evidence of the benefit and ongoing clinical experience for the success of this treatment: Even when these factors were not applied universally. This, combined with the safety of the treatment, makes PRP a compelling treatment worth trying in the appropriate patient.

With time, these factors will be better clarified and likely the success of the treatments will be improved even more.

The potential for a targeted treatment using the body's own capacity to heal itself is an exciting opportunity to explore! There literally is no more "natural" treatment.

BEING HAPPY WITH "GOOD"

Of course, we cannot be happy with good but rather should focus on excellence. Factors which may increase the chance of success includes attempts to eliminate confounding variables, some of which have been addressed in more detail previously. Here we will list some other important factors.

The Road To Excellence:
- Increase accuracy of injection using MSK ultrasound
- Following established pre-and post-protocols regarding activity
- Avoiding anti-inflammatories
- Avoid certain anesthetics which may limit the effectiveness of PRP
- Patient specific factors

- Timing of the injection–not injecting when the patient is presently having a flare of a rheumatic arthritis for example
- **Technique and experience of the physician performing the injection** (is this the 10th, 50th, or 2000th time they have performed procedure?)

WHAT ARE STEM CELLS? AND WHAT ARE NOT?

PRP versus stem cells: PRP is not a stem cell injection. PRP is derived from peripheral blood. What people often refer to as "stem cells" are actually Orthobiologic injections/cellular injections that contain some amount of mesenchymal stem cells. These injections are not pure "stem cells" as they are not cultured stem cells which are then injected. Culturing stem cells, or having cultured stem cells injected is not legal in the United States. For purposes of clarity, we will refer to the bone marrow derived and adipose derived orthobiologic injections containing some mesenchymal stem cells as stem cell injections in this discussion. Stem cells are derived from the patient's own bone marrow or adipose/fat cells. In this sense they are "autologous"

IS PRP "STEM CELL LIGHT?

As noted, PRP is not a stem cell injection. Some people may casually refer to it as a "stem cell type injection". Both PRP and stem cell injections do contain growth factors which have been discussed previously. Growth factors are responsible for the positive effects of the injections, along with the positive inter-molecular signaling provided by interleukins. Besides the fact that stem cell injections have some live mesenchymal stem cells, stem cell injections also have a much higher concentration of growth factors than PRP, as well as much higher concentration of interleukins and other cellular factors.

> **" There** is some promising data with exciting results from stem cells, but much of the data and studies are from small number studies, or even animal models, so this remains an emerging area of study. **"**

ARE "STEM CELL INJECTIONS" BETTER THAN PRP FOR ALL CONDITIONS?

This is a rapidly evolving, emerging area of science and we do not presently have all these answers. One issue is that there are no trials to compare the effectiveness of stem cell injections versus PRP for a given condition. Another issue is that PRP may have favorable data and experience with certain conditions, however stem cell injections have not yet been studied as well for all conditions in comparison to PRP. This is partly because PRP has been available for a longer time in a refined, commercially available manner, and the cost of PRP is significantly less than stem cell injections. For these many reasons, there is a lot more information, experience, and data regarding PRP versus stem cell injections.

There is some promising data with exciting results from stem cells, but much of the data and studies are from small number studies, or even animal models, so this remains an emerging area of study.

The theory is that stem cell injections may be required for a more significant tendon issue, or more advanced cases of arthritis, especially when there is more severe ligament or cartilage injury/damage. Conversely for a "normal case" of tendon or muscle injury, or early osteoarthritis, it may be much more practical, cost efficient, and logical to try PRP first. Ultimately, the decision is up to the individual patient. Some patients may prefer to approach their given issue with a stem cell injection in order that they not only get the advantage of higher overall growth factors, but also live mesenchymal stem cells.

FERTILIZER AND SEEDS

Some have used the analogy of PRP being fertilizer put down on the field that has bald spots and some weeds. In the case of arthritis, just like a field with weeds, there may be a need down the road to do another treatment of fertilizer in order to maintain the health of the field. Stem cell injections meanwhile may be thought of as seeds and fertilizer together, with the mesenchymal stem cells being thought of as actual seeds for the field.

WHAT ARE NOT STEM CELLS?

Some patients may attend a sales type seminar (this should be an immediate warning sign) and hear about amniotic or placental derivative injections being called "stem cell injections." These are NOT stem cell injections and the FDA is quite clear on this subject as well. These types of injections involve dehydrated or freeze-dried membrane grafts (not living cells so they are, by definition, not stem cells.)

These injections do contain certain growth factors and may have some role to play/application in the realm of regenerative medicine and Orthobiologic medicine. Some patients may have very low platelet counts or may have very challenging situations to allow blood draws, therefore these may be considerations for these types of injections. However, these injections should never be referred to as "stem cell" injections.

Presently, these types of injections have scant to no comparative studies, and vastly less data behind their use than PRP. They may have a certain role to play, however this is not well-defined at this time. One advantage to this type of injection is that the injections can be ordered in vials that are reconstituted later with sterile saline. This makes the injection easier to perform for the doctor as there is no need to do blood draw and processing/preparation of the sample. Some patients may be seeking these types of injections and have their own beliefs or interest in these types of injections. This area and many other areas continue to be an area of focus in study presently.

IF I AM OLDER DOES MY BONE MARROW STILL MAKE STEM CELLS?

The simple answer is yes. It follows simple logic and science that the immune response of a healthy young person will be greater than a less healthy/older person. However, the concept that that there will not be a positive immune response because there are not any stem cells present in the bone marrow is typically based on the premise of the natural age-related, fatty degeneration of long bones which occurs naturally with time.

Bone marrow derived stem cell injections are typically taken from the posterior iliac crest (this is the posterior pelvis and not anatomically the hip as often referred to by patients). This area not only contains the highest concentration of stem cells but is also less prone to fatty degeneration that is noted elsewhere in the musculoskeletal system (more stable over time as a patient ages). This is also an area that is considered to have a safer approach as compared to other areas, in the sense of avoiding injury to neurovascular structures.

One exception to the posterior pelvis as the usual site to harvest cells may be during a surgery, when it might make more sense from a logistical and safety perspective for a surgeon to harvest stem cells from a bone adjacent, or near to, the site of the surgery being done.

ARE BONE MARROW DERIVED OR ADIPOSE DERIVED STEM CELLS BETTER?

One reason that adipose derived stem cell injections are performed is that there are actually higher overall numbers of stem cells harvested during this type of procedure than there are with bone marrow derived stem cell procedures. The theory is that this should lead to a better response and results. For many years the data on adipose derived stem cells lagged far behind the data on bone marrow derived stem cells.

Over the past several years, more studies have come out, appearing to show equivalent or the same outcomes as bone marrow aspirate injections for some conditions. In some cases it makes most sense to access cells from the tissue(bone) that is more similar to that which is being treated (bone/cartilage/tendon).

Other clinicians may prefer to obtain a larger overall sample of stem cells as can be obtained in some techniques of adipose stem cells, so that they have a better chance of obtaining a positive result or can even treat multiple areas with this larger sample.

This is also an emerging area and no one has all the answers yet. With either treatment, it is likely that technique may play the most important role in the chance of success.

NO ONE CURES ARTHRITIS

This is an important topic to discuss. A patient being presented these options in a sales environment (sign up now for discount!) without work-up including history, physical exam, x-rays and other needed imaging such as ultrasound or MRI should consider this as a major red flag. In addition, any claims to "cure arthritis" with an injection of PRP or stem cells should be treated with considerable skepticism. No one "cures" arthritis. The injection of PRP may be thought of as putting fertilizer down on the field as has been discussed. There may be some benefit to the "weeds"(pain/dysfunction/loss of activity) but is not likely to do anything for the rocky bald spots in the field that are long gone.

In addition, in the case of arthritis, it is probable that this may have to be done again at some point (ideally not for more than a year or even years later) in order to get the "weeds" back under control.

The length of time the treatment lasts will depend on many factors, including:
- Patient age
- Degree of arthritis (Early/ Moderate/ Severe)
- Activity levels
- Other medical conditions, including obesity amongst others.
  Your doctor may be able to discuss this better for each individual patient

Good news is that often in the case of early knee arthritis, there is a very good response that allows patients significant improvement in functional outcome, with increased activity levels, decrease in pain, and decreased need to take anti-inflammatories.

In addition, much like the fertilizer in the field, PRP may slow the progression of arthritis, as compared to treatments which are known to actually harm the joint, especially with repetitive use, such as

> **"In addition, much like the fertilizer in the field, PRP may slow the progression of arthritis, as compared to treatments which are known to actually harm the joint."**

steroid or "cortisone" injections. There also seems to be some slowing of arthritis relative to other injections/ or relative to no injections being done at all. Studies continue to look at these results and long-term/multiyear results are beginning to accumulate.

In either case, just like fertilizer in the field, PRP in the joint does not always work. It appears to work best for certain joints such as the knee compared to others such as the hip. Sometimes there are too many weeds and too many bald spots, and it may be time to pull up the field and start over (joint replacement). Sometimes it does not work, and no one can understand why.

What certainly seems to matter is that this is done in the best way possible with the most accuracy possible, and with an attempt to eliminate as many variables as possible that can decrease the chance of success. The timing of injections, the frequency of injections, getting a good sample PRP in the first place, limiting any factors that may affect the result such as anti-inflammatories or aspirin, not using certain local anesthetics during the injection, and allowing proper offloading and recovery after the injection all make a difference.

THIS SOUNDS COMPLICATED!

There is no question that this is a complicated area involving a lot of discussion and follow-up. Thus, the decision to move forward with any treatment should involve the appropriate work-up and discussion. Having it performed by an experienced doctor, well-versed in the literature and with appropriate level of procedural experience will increase the chance of success. **It should be clear that this discussion and work-up belongs in a doctor's office not at a sales type seminar.**

IF PRP IS TO BE THOUGHT OF AS FERTILIZER, HOW DO WE CONSIDER STEM CELLS?

This was discussed previously. Some in the field of regenerative medicine would consider stem cell injections as the "seeds" to the "fertilizer" of PRP because with stem cell injections one is getting some live mesenchymal stem cells, which are the true "seeds" of cartilage/bone/tendon/muscle. Therefore, many doctors may recommend this treatment for a "field" (joint/tendon) that has more extensive "weeds" and/or bald spots. Much of the same discussion regarding PRP applies here as well. Data and research on stem cells is more evolving/nascent than PRP presently. There is no guarantee of any treatment working just because it might be theoretically "better" for many other reasons stated above. While there are some small studies showing suggestion of actual regrowth of cartilage, possible healing of cartilage defects and/or ligaments, there is no evidence that stem cell injections "cure arthritis"

WHAT ABOUT THE TENDONS THEN?

PRP treatment does not cure arthritis but rather may calm or quiet it down, possibly even slowing it down, and certainly has potential for significant improvement of function and improvement of quality of life (decrease in pain.) Tendon or muscle injuries when treated with PRP, on the other hand, may actually heal. Currently there are studies showing evidence of actual clinical and radiographic (MRI or MSK ultrasound) healing of some tendon/muscle injuries with PRP.

OF COURSE, THIS DOES NOT ALWAYS HAPPEN, AND DEPENDS ON THE VARIETY OF FACTORS INCLUDING BUT NOT LIMITED TO:

- History of the condition/prior treatments including steroids which can result in a much worse condition and decrease chance of success
- Patient specific factors such as age/health/medical history
- Avoiding negative confounding variables as discussed
- Degree of injury
- Accuracy/skill of physician performing injection ("surgical strike" or "Yosemite Sam?")
- Quality of the PRP/sample
- Other factors causing the tendon injury (is there a giant spur sticking like a stalactite into the tendon?)

The "perfect" method of doing anything, including really awesome things like floating in a gigantic, winding lazy river at a hotel on a hot day, will never be completely proven, and may remain a matter of debate. There will always be individual variables and techniques that affect this definition. (Do you float in the tube or beside it, holding onto it to keep cooler, or walk along it, or keep switching back and forth? When in float position, butt down in water, or belly down? Or through tube bouncing inside like a life ring? Beverage choice? Many choices, may need to alternate? Go down the water slide or keep it chill? Solo float or with a bro? Girlfriend/wife? Kids laughing and chasing? Waterproof Bluetooth speaker or not? Get in and out between reading? Or naps? sooo many questions....)

BACK TO PRP.....

It does seem that performing "needling" of the tendon under ultrasound may be helpful in inducing healing. The exact technique of needling, number or frequency of injections, exact type of PRP to be used (including whether it is white cell rich or not) the type of white cells present, amongst other factors, are all questions presently continuing to be studied. This literature continues to work on answers to these questions, and in doing so comes up with sometimes more questions. Such is the nature of science. Those physicians who have extensive experience injecting a variety of conditions may have figured out some of the secrets in technique inherent to particular conditions.

> **"Those physicians who have extensive experience injecting a variety of conditions may have figured out some of the secrets in technique inherent in particular conditions."**

There does seem to be evidence that PRP works better for certain tendon conditions than others as was described. Certain areas have better literature support than others. Ask your doctor what the current literature states about the condition, and what their experience has been. One encouraging trend in the field of orthobiologic medicine has been seeing more collaborative data between multiple clinics/sites, and increasing use of data/outcome registries to try and better define the theoretical likelihood of success, as well as refine the ideal techniques for given conditions, based on a larger field of experience.

GENERAL STATEMENTS

PRP is a promising treatment that presently has favorable outcomes with several conditions, but it is not magic fairy dust. It does not cure arthritis, or magically reconnect a torn rotator cuff, or repair a completely torn ACL, for example. PRP is not going to put good orthopedic surgeons out of business. There will always be a need for surgical treatment of certain conditions. As the cost of healthcare continues to explode with an aging population in the United States, there will be a continued need for other meaningful options for patients. As a society we should be evolving beyond the point of using treatments that are known to be harmful, such as anti-inflammatories and steroid injections, as a basis of our treatment unless there are no other options for a given patient. Some patients may not want surgery. Some conditions, including certain tendon conditions, do not have great surgical outcomes. Some patients are not medical candidates for surgery based on their other medical conditions.

For many of these patients, having an option such as PRP is tremendously helpful.

IS PRP FOR ME?

Standing at a crossroads, with roads heading in different directions, sometimes the signs seem to be written in Sanskrit. The answer may be simple, or it may also be somewhat complicated.

The answer may be NO because it is time to have joint replacement done.

The answer may be NO because you have a contraindication to getting PRP.

The answer may be NO because you are a young athlete with a full thickness ACL tear, and you need surgery to restore function (although interestingly PRP is often used as part of the surgical process in some cases).

There may be other reasons or conditions which would make surgery favorable, especially if other treatments have been tried and did not work.

The famous physician William Osler said, "First make the diagnosis". Do not be confused or despair. Make a consultation with a qualified and experienced doctor and have an evaluation of your history, physical exam, review of prior imaging. Any new imaging that needs to be done can be completed at that time as well. No one can answer the question of whether this treatment is for you without consideration of these factors.

The good news is that if the answer is YES you will be embarking upon an exciting opportunity to use the capacity of your body to result in a natural healing response. You will be avoiding the toxicities of medications and other treatments that we know to be ineffective or even harmful.

SUMMARY:
  Current Data and Experience of the Author:

  When might PRP be best option/highest present evidence & good experience of author:
  - Early Knee OA
  - Medial collateral ligament/MCL
  - Various Tendinopathy including
    - Lateral/medial epicondylitis
    - Plantar fasciitis
    - Achilles tendon
    - Rotator cuff/especially isolated cuff injuries (not full-thickness tears)
    - Hamstring/quadriceps tendinopathy

- Gastrocnemius/calf muscle tendinopathy
- Gluteus Medius tendinopathy (often misdiagnosed as hip bursitis)

Less published evidence/ however good experience of author:
- **Some conditions may have not been as thoroughly studied, but this does not mean this is not a very good option to consider. It has been the experience of the author that these conditions responded very favorably
- De Quervain's tenosynovitis (wrist tendinitis at the top portion of the thumb)
- Hand flexor tendinopathy
- Ulnar collateral ligament partial tear
  - Details of proximal or distal, extent of tear, and timeline of the patient/athlete all very important factors in making this complicated decision

Tougher conditions/ with not as much data, but still good option to consider:
- **Again not "curing arthritis", but injection of PRP may be far more favorable than steroid injections which can be very short lasting; lead to further degeneration of the joint, soft tissue atrophy or depigmentation, and elevation of blood sugars, amongst many issues. It has been the experience of the author that PRP injections may provide significant functional relief of pain, and patients sometimes get lasting relief for 12+ months which is tremendous!
- Ankle arthritis
- Carpometacarpal/CMC arthritis (base of thumb: Most common joint and body to get arthritis)

- Hallux rigidus (arthritis of the big toe resulting in stiffness and significant pain)
- Glenohumeral arthritis (shoulder joint)
- Acromioclavicular joint arthritis ("point" of the shoulder)

The Toughest Conditions/ Data is conflicting/ most challenging for author also:
- Patellar tendon
  - Challenging condition, comprehensive approach required including extensive physical therapy
  - Technique may be very important, there are some papers published describing specific technique when injecting "Patellar scraping"
- Hip/labrum and hip arthritis
  - Neither the literature nor author's experience provides the same level of result in comparison to the knee.
  - Still may be the best option for patient that is not ready for surgery.
  - Candid conversation a must.
- Important to make sure that the source of the pain is clearly identified, and it is not being referred from the back, or some of the muscles around the hip joints

---

Emerging Areas showing some promise:
- Peripheral nerve
- Technique also key here, doing "hydrodissection" under MSK US to "free up" nerve from entrapment. May be additional benefit of growth factors from PRP on nerve tissue
- Spine/intradiscal
- Technique and experience also paramount. May require use of

fluoroscopy or other imaging for appropriate guidance. Often doctors who inject this area may specialize in the spine/ or do mostly spine injections

HOW DO WE DEFINE SUCCESS?

Success may be defined as an improvement in clinical outcome or function. No one who gets PRP is going to hear fairies sparkling in the air and then wake up the next day, and they are 20 years younger. This is not magic fairy dust. It is a valid treatment however, with increasing levels of data and success. I have literally performed thousands of treatments with excellent results, and I count myself as extremely blessed to have an opportunity to see so many patients have such good results. Seeing patients return to improved levels of activity and have improvement in their quality of life, decrease in pain, and regain a sense of wellbeing and vigor makes me profoundly happy. In addition, knowing that many of these patients are not exposing themselves to the negative effects of anti-inflammatory medications, and by moving and being more active are decreasing their overall health risks is an added benefit.

My definition of success is excellent care and guidance to a patient on this journey, whether or not it is I that performs the treatment or another appropriate physician. **That is my PRP roadmap to success.**

ACKNOWLEDGEMENTS:

To my wife Stephanie for her support, friendship, and love.

To Emma Aislinn, Liam Eamonn, and Lily Aibhlinn for their love, laughter, and making me long for home. Riamh géilleadh.

To all of those I have learned from: attendings in my training, and fellows/residents/students who relight the spark as time moves on. We can all learn a bit if we occasionally listen to each other.

Thank you to Ross Jobson (Faircount Publishing) for edits and being a good friend/brother.
www.faircount.com

Thank you to Robin McDowall of McDowall Design for the brilliant layout and design.
www.mcdowalldesign.com

Thank you to my practice staff for understanding that the right answer always lies in what is best for the patient, and for caring enough to want to be excellent - not just good.

GLOSSARY OF TERMS:

Anesthetics: Class of medications used to decrease or dull pain. In the setting of injections, sometimes given prior to the injection being used for treatment to provide adequate ability to approach the tendon or joint structure.

Autologous: Derived from self/ not another organism. Examples of autologous orthobiologics include PRP, BMA/BMAC, and Adipose derived stem cells.

BMA/BMAC: Bone marrow aspirate derived from patient, typically the posterior iliac crest (posterior pelvis). This site considered to be a safer approach and contains the highest concentration of bone marrow derived mesenchymal stem cells in the body, and also remains more stable throughout life, undergoing less fatty degeneration which occurs in long bones. Bone marrow aspirate concentrate is bone marrow aspirate which is then minimally manipulated/spun down in a centrifuge to obtain a concentrate of bone marrow derived stem cells.

Cellular Therapy: The field of Ortho Biologics (see def) comprised of injections derived from active cellular materials, to include PRP, BMAC, BMA, adipose derived mesenchymal stem cells, and possibly amniotic and placental products, although amniotic and placental products do not contain live cellular materials.

Corticosteroid: Synthetic drugs developed to try and mimic the action of "cortisol", a hormone produced by the adrenal gland. Patients often refer to steroid injections as "cortisone injections". Common examples of steroid injections used are methylprednisone, triamcinolone, betamethasone, and dexamethasone. These medications have similar actions, but may have different water solubility and half lives.

Hemodynamic Instability: Term indicating relative dysfunction and instability related to low blood counts (anemia) or low blood pressure causing relative decreased blood flow to vital organs.

HgB/Hemoglobin: "Red blood cell" or "RBC". Cells produced in the bone marrow which are used to carry oxygen and support life. Measure of hemoglobin sometimes referred by patients as "red blood count".

Leukocyte: "White blood cell" or "WBC". Cellular component made in the bone marrow which have various types, but are used by the body to fight and counter disease and insult.

Leukocyte Rich PRP: Term used to refer to PRP which has presence of white blood cells in the sample. This does not refer to the type of white blood cells. At present, research seems to indicate that leukocyte rich PRP is more favorable for tendon related issues rather than joint. There is probably specific types of white cells within the white cell component that are particularly better than others for these processes and this is an ongoing area of research.

Leukocyte poor PRP: Term used to refer to PRP which has the absence of white blood cells in the sample. At present, research seems to indicate that leukocyte poor PRP is more favorable for joint applications.

Mesenchymal Stem Cells: MSCs: Multipotent stromal cells capable of differentiating into a variety of cell types. Present in multiple tissues, including bone marrow, adipose tissue, and the umbilical cord. These cells can self-renew by dividing and differentiate into various tissues including bone, muscle, connective tissue.

Monocyte: Types of white cells or leukocytes which may differentiate/turn into macrophages which are types of white cells used in immune defense and cleaning up cellular material.

MSK US: Musculoskeletal ultrasound. Imaging done real-time with active/dynamic movement, providing accuracy and supported by literature to provide superior outcomes with injections.

NSAIDs: Nonsteroidal anti-inflammatory drugs. Common examples in Table 2. These drugs act by inhibiting pathways which produce inflammatory mediators. Generally used to decrease or mask pain.

Neutrophil: Types of white cells or leukocytes used in the immune system response. These are the most plentiful type of white blood cell. Recruited to the sites of injury quickly after trauma or injury, and are the hallmark of acute inflammation. They may however cause negative effects in a joint application, so many in the field of orthobiologics try to use a leukocyte poor preparation in these cases.

Orthobiologics: Treatments used in a musculoskeletal applications of joint and tendon/muscle derived from biologically active products used to help heal injuries more quickly or decrease pain. These substances are found naturally in the body.

Platelets: Small cellular components which are made in the bone marrow. These cells help with clotting, and also produce the growth factors which are involved in cellular processes and healing.

PRP: Platelet rich plasma. Cellular sample obtained by minimal manipulation/centrifuge separating the whole blood component into a red blood cells, platelet poor plasma, and the buffy coat or platelet rich plasma. In general, many in the field of Ortho Biologics consider PRP to be a sample which contains at least 6 times that of whole blood. Samples which contain lower concentrates might be referred to as "autologous conditioned plasma" not platelet rich plasma.

Septicemia: Also referred to as blood poisoning/ it is a cascade of events related to a severe illness or infections whereby chemicals are released into the blood stream cause organ disfunction and failure.

Tendon: A tendon is a structure which binds a muscle to the bone. Tendons are under great stress from the force placed upon them and also have relatively poor blood flow which makes them susceptible to injury.

Thrombocytopenia: Term referring to low platelet counts. This may lead to difficulty controlling bleeding or even spontaneous bleeding. Lower platelet counts may affect the ability to concentrate platelets for PRP. It is not well understood what the absolute number must be at a baseline in order to still have a positive effect.

QUICK TABLES/ "HIGH YIELD" QUICK REFS:

TABLE 1: RISKS OF ANTI INFLAMMATORIES (NSAIDS):

Risks/ problems with anti-inflammatories

- Gastrointestinal issues such as ulcers and gastritis
- Cardiovascular risks, such as hypertension, increased rates of congestive heart failure and an increase in risk of heart attack and stroke, issues of increased edema
- Kidney damage and compromise-especially in older patients,
- All of these risks despite not actually doing anything to slow or change the course of the osteoarthritis itself.
- Recent studies show evidence of slowing of bone healing in animal models in the case of fractures which brings further questions to the table about this class of medications.

TABLE 2: COMMON ANTI INFLAMMATORIES (NSAIDS)

Some common over the counter or prescription anti-inflammatories include:

- aspirin
- Motrin
- Aleve
- Naprosyn
- naproxen
- Voltaren
- Advil
- ibuprofen
- meloxicam
- Mobic
- Celebrex
- Daypro
- Feldene
- Lodine
- Lodine
- Ansaid

It is also vital that prednisone and any other corticosteroid injections are discontinued 3 weeks prior and as many as 4 weeks post the injection.

TABLE 3: THE HEALING CASCADE
Understanding PRP involves understanding the Healing Cascade

Hemostasis
- Clot formation to degranulation of platelets-this involves stopping the acute bleeding

Acute inflammatory phase
- Can last up to 72 hours-characterized by pain, swelling, redness and increased local temperature.

Intermediate repair phase
- 48 hours to 6 weeks
- Anatomic structures restored and tissue regeneration occurring
- Fibroblasts, angiogenesis-activity of the growth factors is seen on the tissues

Advanced remodeling phase
- 3 weeks to 12 months
- Collagen remodeling

TABLE 4: FACTORS THAT AFFECT THE SUCCESS OF PRP:
Factors that affect the success of the PRP include

- Which tendon/injury is being treated
- How long or how badly the tendon is injured
- Specific techniques of procuring and or performing PRP itself including the skill of the clinician
- Possibly "dose" of the PRP, including number of injections required to achieve the positive result
- Patient factors including
  - Age
  - Health with patient, possibly baseline platelet counts
- Type of PRP being used
- Kinetic chain issues as previously discussed
- Avoiding confounding variables which may affect the success of PRP
  - Recent anti-inflammatory use or steroid use
  - Possible inactivation or effect on the PRP by certain local anesthetics
  - Appropriate offloading and activity modification after injection

TABLE 5: WHAT TO LOOK FOR IN THE PHYSICIAN PERFORMING YOUR PRP

What to Look for in Your Physician?

Having this or any procedure done is a big decision, and there are certain things that a patient should look for when deciding which doctor to see for an initial consultation:

- Is the doctor board certified?
- Is an appropriate workup being done/ or just signing up to do injections?
- Experience of doctor? (Everyone starts somewhere, but technical skill with anything increases with time and experience. Having done hundreds of injections is much better than dozens)
- Is MSK US used for guidance of injection? (If not, like taking a shot in the dark. "Guessing" where it is going)
- Is an MD/DO performing the injection? (Some clinics may recruit patients and then have a mid-level practitioner (ARNP or PA) actually performing the injections who may or may not use MSK US or have any expertise with it for that matter)
- What is the process? (Assembly line of injections with no follow up or are there solid follow up plans made?)
- Instructions provided/ ability to ask questions?
- Familiarity of the doctor with the literature?
- Feedback from other patients/ reviews?

TABLE 6: SOME NATURAL WAYS TO BOOST HEALTH/PREPARE FOR INJECTION:

Night Before/Morning of:
- Get a good night's sleep,
- Stay off "Dr. Google"
- Avoid anti-inflammatories
- Drink plenty of water (8 glasses of 8 oz for example)
- Eat a good breakfast
- Breathe, good positive energy

Leading up to Injection:
- Eating fruits and nuts that have less inflammatory properties
- blueberries, apples, blackberries, raspberries, strawberries, pecans, almonds
- Less/ no meats or at least lean meats
- chicken, lamb, fresh fish, or turkey
- Drinking black coffee, herbal teas, fresh juices over caffeinated sodas or processed sugar-containing drinks
- Healthy, fresh vegetables, limit or avoid alcohol

NO SMOKING!

Other Ideas to Stimulate Health may include:
- Improved sleep quality
- Trying to manage stress, avoiding blue lights before bed, sleep hygiene-avoiding caffeine so there is more good quality sleep.
- Avoiding fast foods + processed foods that contain high degrees of sugar
- Avoiding high degrees of saturated fats
- Exercise is medicine...!
- In general exercise and motion can help bring blood flow to an area, movement is important.
- Managing stress, stress leads to cortisol release, cortisol is a toxic hormone.
- Self-care which may include meditation, yoga, prayer
- Managing any other known inflammatory conditions for example if history of inflammatory arthritis trying to control it/in consultation with other doctors/ rheumatology

TABLE 7: CONTRAINDICATIONS TO PRP

What are contraindications to PRP?

Absolute contraindications include:

- Platelet dysfunction syndrome
- Critical thrombocytopenia
- Hemodynamic instability
- Septicemia
- Local infection at the site of the procedure/ or open skin
- Patient unwilling to accept risks/ and or costs of procedure

Relative contraindications include:

- Consistent use of NSAIDs prior to the procedure (especially within 48 hours/ but maybe as long as 5 days)
- Corticosteroid injection at the treatment site within 1 month
- Systemic use of steroids within 4 weeks
- Tobacco use
- Recent fever or illness
- Cancer- especially of blood or bone derived
- HgB 10 g/dl
- Platelet count < 105

TABLE 8: THE ROAD TO EXCELLENCE: THE BEST RESULTS FROM PRP

The road to excellence:

- Increase accuracy of injection using MSK ultrasound
- Following established pre-and post-protocols regarding activity
- Avoiding anti-inflammatories
- Avoid using anesthetics which may limit the effectiveness of PRP
- Patient specific factors
- Timing of the injection-not injecting when the patient is presently having a flare of a rheumatic arthritis for example
- Technique and experience of the physician performing the injection (is this the 10th, 50th, or 2000th time they have injected?)

TABLE 9: THE ROAD TO EXCELLENCE: THE BEST RESULTS FROM PRP

The road to excellence:

- History of the condition/prior treatments including steroids which can result in a much worse condition and decrease chance of success
- Patient specific factors such as age/health/medical history
- Avoiding negative confounding variables as discussed
- Degree of injury
- Accuracy/skill of physician performing injection ("surgical strike" or "Yosemite Sam?")
- Quality of the PRP/sample
- Other factors causing the tendon injury (is there giant spur sticking likely still like tight into the tendon?)

TABLE 10: WHEN IS PRP BEST OPTION:
(Good Literature Support and Experience of Author)
Early Knee OA

Medial collateral ligament/MCL

Various Tendinopathy including

- Lateral/medial epicondylitis
- Plantar fasciitis
- Achilles tendon
- Rotator cuff/especially isolated cuff injuries (not full-thickness tears)
- Hamstring/quadriceps tendinopathy
- Gastrocnemius/calf muscle tendinopathy
- Gluteus Medius tendinopathy (often misdiagnosed as hip bursitis)

TABLE 11: STRONG CONSIDERATIONS FOR PRP: LESS STUDIED IN LITERATURE/BUT GOOD EXPERIENCE OF AUTHOR
De Quervain's tenosynovitis (wrist tendinitis at the top portion of the thumb)

Hand flexor tendinopathy

Ulnar collateral ligament partial tear

- Details of proximal or distal, extent of tear, and timeline of the patient/athlete all very important factors in making this complicated decision

TABLE 12: TOUGH CONDITIONS THAT PRP MAY HELP DECREASE PAIN, IMPROVE FUNCTION
Ankle arthritis

Carpometacarpal/CMC arthritis (base of thumb: Most common joint and body to get arthritis)

Hallux rigidus (arthritis of the big toe resulting in stiffness and significant pain)

Glenohumeral arthritis (shoulder joint)

Acromioclavicular joint arthritis ("point" of the shoulder)

LUCKY #13: DECISION TREE FOR LAZY RIVERS

Does Hotel Have a Lazy River?

YES — NO

Is it open? — Leave

NO

Leave

YES

Is it hot?

YES — NO

Inner tubes — Heated Pool

YES — NO — YES — NO

Sit on steps and wait or go commando without one — Don't be soft

Options
A: Grab one
B: Lots available—make a floating palace

Beverages
"Hydration is key", but no glass
A: Insulated tumbler at chair/in and out might lose tube
B: Tucked in safe positions at corner

Float posture

A: Butt down – good vantage point, stay cool, can keep hat and sunglasses out of water

B: Stomach down – easier exit if chasing kids, may want to even out sun exposure/etc.

C. Life ring float.
Can bob along, fun
Con-larger humans may get stuck, not easy exit

D. Holding on side of tube
-not versatile
-may be better able to avoid sun exposure

E. Multiple tubes
-plenty of options abound
-most labor intensive

Water slide

YES   NO

Really hot   Cool, more
or have   chill time
kids?   in lazy
                    river

YES   NO

Take a   Might skip
turn and
try it.

Company

A: Solo floater – form of meditation

B: Bro's/etc – conversation

C: Significant other couples float, holding hands/tubes, linked feet, holding on each other's tube

Music

A: No – listen to the birds, meditate

B: Bro's/etc – conversation

C: loud pool and lots of chaos – may need chill vibe to prevent panic attack

In and out of pool

A: Water + sun = naps // naps + lazy river = nirvana

B: Big session then naps – lessens chance of losing tube

PRP

A Roadmap for Success©

Kevin Edward Elder, MD, FAAFP, has extensive experience with musculoskeletal ultrasound and was one of the first physicians in the Tampa Bay area performing this diagnostic evaluation on patients, as well as one of the first physicians in the area performing PRP. He has lectured extensively on this topic and has several publications in this area as well. He has performed over 3000 PRP injections and continues to work on perfecting the process.

Printed in Poland
by Amazon Fulfillment
Poland Sp. z o.o., Wrocław